Observi

by Anna Schlecker

PEARSON
Scott Foresman

DK

What is matter?

Matter takes up space.

It has **mass.**

It has tiny parts.

Some parts are too small to see.

Describing Matter

Matter can have different shapes.
It can have different sizes.
How are the things in this picture alike and different?

What are solids, liquids, and gases?

A **solid** is matter.

It takes up space.

A solid does not change shape.

A **liquid** is matter.

This liquid takes the shape of the bottle.

A liquid takes the shape of what it is in.

A liquid's size does not change.

A **gas** is matter.

It takes up space.

It can change size and shape.

It takes the shape of what it is in.

Bubbles are filled with air.

Air is a gas.

How does matter change?

Matter can change.

It can change in many ways.

A liquid can freeze when it is cold.

A solid can melt when it is hot.

Mixing Solids and Liquids

Soup is made of solids and liquids. The solids and liquids are mixed. You can take the solids out of the liquid.

Some solids dissolve in liquids.
Dissolve means to spread
throughout a liquid.

How can water change?

Water is a liquid.

Water can freeze when it gets cold.

The water changes to ice.

Ice is a solid.

Heat melts ice.

The ice changes to water.

Water boils when it gets very hot.

The water changes to a gas.

This gas is water vapor.

What are other ways matter changes?

Heat makes water evaporate.

Evaporate means to change from liquid to gas.

The Sun can make water on the ground evaporate.

Paper is a solid.

Paper can burn.

It will not turn back into paper.

Matter is all around us.

It can change.

Glossary

dissolve	to spread throughout a liquid
evaporate	to change from a liquid to a gas
gas	matter that can change size and shape
liquid	matter that has its own size and takes the shape of its container
mass	the amount of matter in an object
matter	anything that takes up space
solid	matter that has its own shape and size